Also available by Denar Ralph

Climbing The Ladder To Success: Just A Little Inspiration
ISBN 978-1-387-40476-6

# The Daily Climb:
## 31 Days of **Inspiration** **To** Help You **Climb** Your Ladder To Success

Dedicated to my parents:

Patricia Ralph

and

Denroy Ralph

The words "Thank You!" are not enough

# The Daily Climb: 31 Days of Inspiration To Help You Climb Your Ladder To Success

Published by
## Denar Ralph Publishing
Copyright 2018. Denar Ralph

All rights reserved.

No part of this book may be reproduced without permission, except for brief quotations in books and critical reviews.

All the names and many of the locations have changed to protect the identities of the innocent and the guilty.

For more information about
## Denar Ralph Publishing
Contact:

Patricia and Denroy Ralph

patralph10@gmail.com

917-870-8214

917-324-0567

ISBN 978-0-359-26898-6

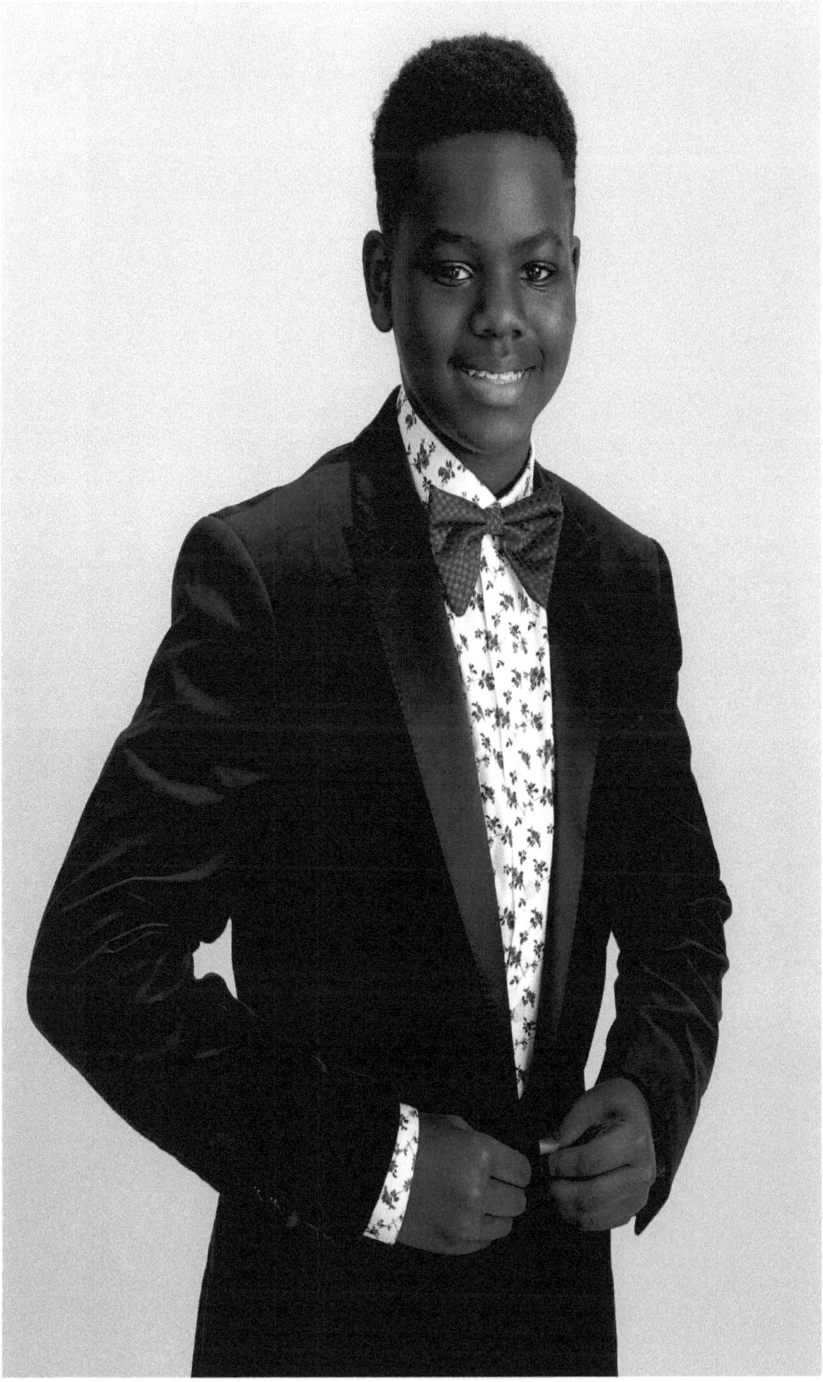

## PREFACE

Denar, the youngest of four children, was born on January 7, 2005. His dream is to attend Harvard University to pursue a degree in law. Denar, a luminary, published his first book in 2017 "Climbing the Ladder to Success." He is engaged in motivational speaking to inspire the youths. Letting them know, they too, can climb the ladder to the next positive level in their life and claim their purpose.

Denar is doing just that, multifaceted, he continues to claim his purpose in life. He owns and manages his business, "Denar Ralph Origami Floral Arrangements." An artist, he creates floral arrangements for weddings, church banquets, and parties; using an ancient tradition of Japanese art call Origami. He sings, and plays several musical instruments, the piano, the keyboard and the steel drums. His message to youths is simple, you can claim your purpose in life at a young age. I am confident, that Climbing the Ladder to Success will positively impact this young generation.

by Patricia Ralph (*aka Mom*)

# Introduction

I am extremely grateful and humbled to again be in such a position to inspire people through my writing. In my previous book, I was contacted by so many people telling me about how that book touched, inspired, and motivated them to continue their climb up the ladder to success.

It's a fact that it takes about 21 days to turn a practice into a habit. This is the challenge I am giving you now. I want to take your success to another level. My previous book inspired my readers that they can do anything they put their mind to. I was able to do this by explaining how I achieved my own success. Like countless others before me, the lessons I learned came from: my life experiences, the things I've seen, the people I've met, and the places I've visited.

In this book, I will help you turn your successes into a regular habit. I want it to become part of your lifestyle. I made this book to assist you in climbing your ladder to success. I have gone beyond the 21 days to develop a habit into a 31 day challenge because I want you to develop perseverance <u>and</u> fortitude.

Never give up!! This is the mentality that I want you to develop. This will take you higher in life. Think of "Never give up!" as a key to every locked door in your life. But it's not enough that you simply read about this key. You have to take it up and use it. So as you begin this portion of your climb to success, let every day take you closer to your destination. And when you finally make it, don't forget to thank God and your family!

# Day 1
# Being A Winner

Being a winner is not about being the best, the first, or the greatest. Being a winner is about accomplishing things. Winners get it done. In my relatively short time on this planet, I have accomplished many things in my life. These things include;
- Writing a book ,
- Owning a business
- Establishing a non-profit organization.

Webster's dictionary defines a winner as "someone who achieves victory in a game, competition, or election." I think this definition is missing something very important. In life, there are two types of winners:
- one who actually wins something
- one who makes their dreams a reality

Someone who makes their dreams come true is a true winner. Only a true winner can have that drive, motivation, and determination to dream and to take it further by making it a reality. It is easy to sleep and dream, but hard to get up and make it come true. So when you do make your dreams come true, it says a lot about you. It shows that you are independent and strong minded.

Another thing you must remember is that no one can share your dream. Your dream is personal. Winners find ways of making their dreams come true and are not dependent on anyone to make it happen for them. If you wait for people to make your dreams come true, then you are only holding yourself back from ever being successful.

So after reading this, dare to dream, then dare to make it a reality.

**Understand:** In the space provided below, write how being a winner, and not just a dreamer, can help you climb the ladder to success.

_____
_____
_____
_____
_____
_____
_____
_____
_____
_____
_____
_____
_____
_____
_____
_____
_____

# Day 2
# Positive Thinking

It's a good thing to always have and maintain a positive mindset. The problems in life are only a test. Maintaining a positive mindset through these problems will build a high self-esteem. Without a positive mindset our thoughts have put us in a self-destructive losing pattern. It looks like this:
- People with a negative mindset are easily stressed
- People who give in to stress develop low self-esteem
- People with low self-esteem develop negative mindsets
- And the cycle continues...

A negative mindset causes a person to focus on all the bad things instead of the good things. This is true, especially in the morning. When you wake up, it is crucial to have a positive mindset because you can either make an impact on the world or the world will have an impact on you. Keep a positive attitude.

My suggestion is to do at least three acts of kindness every day. This small contribution of kindness can change the world for the better. This is all because of your decision to make an impact with your actions.

So, today, I challenge you to act!

**Understand:** In the space provided below, list some acts of kindness that you can do today and how it can help you climb the ladder to success.

_____

_____

_____

# Day 3
# The Power of Forgiveness

It is easier to judge a person on their outward appearance, rather than what is on the inside. It is also easier to condemn someone for what that person did in the past, than to compliment them for what they are doing today. In the same way, you wouldn't want anyone to profile you based on your past mistakes, therefore you shouldn't do it to others. Do not be the kind of person that uses past incidents to hold another person back from all that they can become in the future. Always remember, your present decisions will not only affect your future, but others as well.

If you decide to treat others with love and compassion, then love and compassion will follow you into the future. There are many instances where it is hard to not judge someone based off of what they've done to you. Just like the reason I explained, if someone sincerely and truly apologizes to you, you have to forgive them.

Another point is this... you shouldn't let your past problems define what you are capable of now. It's Just like a baby learning how to walk. When a baby starts to crawl and begins to attempt to walk, there is a very high chance that the baby is going to fall. This doesn't stop them! Sometimes the baby will even begin laughing after they fell down, but they always get back up and try again!!

So, today, I dare you to forgive someone and to live in the present. This is the best way to fully unleash what you are capable of doing today.

**Understand:** In the space provided below, write how can you live in the present and how can it help you climb the ladder to success.

_____

_____

# Day 4
# Answer Your Calling

Always do what you love. Just as long as what you love is taking you higher up the ladder to success. Don't let anyone tell you what you are meant to be. You are not limited by their thoughts. For instance, if you love baking cakes, then bake cakes! If you love technology, then pursue technology. Don't let anyone stop you. As I stated previously, your success is personal. Beware and be aware of negative influences around you. When you do see them around you, immediately dismiss them from your presence. Don't even waste time thinking about them. If anyone is telling you that you can't do something, don't believe it. Just prove that you can with your actions backing up your words and dreams. Many people ask me, "Is your mission to inspire people to write their own books?" My answer is always the same. "No. I am not. I'm inspiring people to pursue their dreams."
If you believe you are called to be an author, then do it. You just need to have the motivation to do it. The only way to know your callings is to make sure it's something you love doing and have a passionate desire to do.

So, today, I challenge you to find out what you love to do and then go do it!!

**Understand:** In the space provided below, write the things you love doing and how these things you love can help you climb the ladder to success.

_____

_____

_____

_____

# Day 5
## Changing The World

People may wonder, how can I make an impact on the world? Well, believe it or not, I think I have a pretty good answer. The answer is to "Start small". Just a small good deed can touch millions and millions of people. You have the power to be an inspiration to others. Greeting a stranger with the words "Good morning!" can impact the rest of their day. Never keep your power of inspiration to yourself. It was yours to give away not keep. Plus, you're not going to change the world, if you don't start with the small things.

This world would be a much better place, if we all shared inspiration. I like to think of it as gas for a car. Inspiration is like the fuel for the car to keep you going through the day. What would happen if no one ever gave you a drop of the inspirational fuel you need to make it through the day. How far in life are you really going to go? This illustration is just to show you that whenever you have a good word or a good deed or something good that you want to express, don't wait to express it. That little word or deed or thing can change someone's life and be the first step in changing the world.

So, today, I challenge you to be an agent of change and make an impact.

**Understand:** In the space provided below, write how can you change the world and how this can help everybody you know begin to climb the ladder to success.

_____

_____

# Day 6
# Embrace Your Imperfections

Has anybody ever called you weird? Or have you ever felt that you're not pretty enough? Normally this is a bad thing, but it doesn't have to be. By pointing out your imperfections, people are only pointing out what makes you special. For example, let's say you are working with wood and you get a splinter in your hand, but the splinter stays lodged inside. After days of discomfort, the splinter is eventually removed but a scar remains behind. This is true about life. Everything we go through in life will leave behind some kind of evidence. Every scar has a story. It may tell the story of a cut, a burn, or a scrape, but every scar is a reminder of something we have overcome and healed from. When people look at this cut that you have on your hand you can proudly say, "I got it because I was working hard."

Sometimes our scars are beneath the surface. Some things scar us emotionally. People might look at you and call you weird because of your way of living. But don't let it get you down. Your way of doing things is what makes you unique. No one else expresses them self the way you do. Never be afraid to be you. Learn to express yourself whether be talking or writing or dancing or singing or doing art.

So, today, I challenge you to discover whatever make you unique and celebrate it.

**Understand:** In the space provided below, write what makes you unique and describe how your imperfections help you climb the ladder to success.

# Day 7
# The Power Of The Word "Can't"

If only people knew about the negative power of the word "can't". That word always has an impact on somebody's life. It's time to remove it from your vocabulary. The word "can't" prevents the next great thing from happening. The word can't has the power to cripple and debilitate a person their whole life.

Has anyone ever told you that you can't do something? How did it affect you? Did it help you become who you are today? Or did it stunt you from growing? If someone ever tells you that you can't accomplish something, then turn that word into "can". This is not an easy task. When somebody tells me that I can't do something, and it's something that I am passionate about doing, I turn it into fuel to empower me. I use it to motivate me. I say I can do anything I can put my mind to, as long as I have a positive mindset and determination.

So, today, I challenge you to look back on all the things people told you that you would never be able to do in life and then go out and do it to the best of your ability.

**Understand:** In the space provided below, write what you can do and how this can help you climb the ladder to success.

_____

_____

_____

_____

# Day 8
# Stop Taking The Shortcut

In today's world, it is very easy to take shortcuts or to be lazy. This is especially true in the times that we are living. Technology makes things very easy. However, many of us don't understand that when we take shortcuts, we are not getting anything out of it .

Many people say, "All that matters is the destination", but they are wrong. The lesson is in the journey. There are certain things in life that you can only find in the journey. You won't get this if you rush to the destination. The advantages that come from hard work and experience can only be found in the journey and are what you will need once you reach the destination. You will not get it if you take the shortcut.

So, today, I challenge you to go for the journey. In spite of the temptation to take the shorter route, keep a steadfast mind and go the distance.

**Understand:** In the space provided below, write some things you can learn on the journey (example- patience). In doing this, how can this help you climb the ladder to success?

_____

_____

_____

_____

# Day 9
# Learn From Your Mistakes

It can be very hard to learn from mistakes. I say this because the first step of learning from your mistake is acknowledging that your are only human and not perfect in any way, shape, or form. Humility plays a big role in this. It takes a lot of humility to acknowledge that you have made a mistake. This seemingly simple advice is very hard for many to follow for many. This is because a person must first admit his or her weaknesses and then act on what he or she observed. Without acting upon our analysis, we are starting back at the bottom of the ladder all over again. Simply because we didn't apply what we learned.

This is why learning from your mistakes is a learning opportunity. Whatever you failed to do in the past, is now a chance to fix. You have a second chance to work at it. You can see the new results this time.

**Understand:** In the space provided below, write what mistakes of the past you can make right and how this can help you climb the ladder to success.

_____

_____

_____

_____

_____

# Day 10
## Don't Doubt Your Calling

When trouble comes, a lot of people start to doubt their calling. Instead of envisioning success, they can only see problems and start to back away in fear. They start to believe that they were never "called" to succeed. Don't let your thoughts get you down. When you answer your call, you shouldn't be worried about problems. Even not having enough money shouldn't make you doubt. When you find something that you really want to do, don't be afraid to ask for help.

Your calling is what you personally want to do. It is not what anybody else wants you to do. So, whenever you find yourself in a situation where you start questioning your calling or what you want to do, just remind yourself that you can do anything you put your mind. Set your mind to thinking positive thoughts.

So, today, I dare you to answer your calling. If it's something that you are not capable of doing individually, I challenge you to be humble and ask for help.

**Understand**: In the space provided below, answer this question: How does pursuing my dream help me climb the ladder to success?

_____

_____

_____

_____

# Day 11
# Be Bigger Than Your Circumstances

In life, we are going to eventually be in a situation where you going to be challenged by your circumstance. In these instances, you are going to have to rise above them. Usually I would say, "Be like a chameleon and adapt to your circumstances", but today is different. Instead of being like a chameleon, I want to you to be like a hermit crab. A hermit crab is often overlooked but it is a power creature. When it grows too big for its shell, it goes off in search of another one.

Many of us have stuffed ourselves into shells of routine and tradition. We miss out on the joys of life and become unable to work to our fullest potential. When life becomes a pattern of simply: get up, go out, and come home, then it's definitely time to find a new shell. In doing so, you will be able to live more fully in life. Not a life that chooses to please others, but a life where you are comfortable pleasing yourself.

When a hermit crab goes out to find a bigger shell, I'm sure it's not easy. Finding success in life is not easy, but it's definitely worth the effort. The hardest part of breaking a habit is actually doing it. So don't be discouraged, if you find it difficult to do this.

So, today, I encourage you and challenge you to do something new. Get out of your comfort zone. When you become bigger than your circumstances, go out and find a new shell.

**Understand**: In the space provided below, write some ways you can come out of your uncomfortable situation and how it help you climb up the ladder to success.

_____

_____

_____

_____

_____

_____

_____

_____

_____

_____

_____

_____

_____

_____

_____

_____

# Day 12
# Your Calling Makes You Unique

What you do makes you special. Even if you consider what you do is very simple. No matter what it is, it makes you unique. Let's use an example of a family. Suppose you are a street sweeper but everyone in your family is a lawyer. Don't let others control what you want to do, even if what you do makes you look inferior to others. Not everyone wants to grow up to be a street sweeper. This is why it makes you unique. The true meaning of unique is being different. In doing so, it might make you look as if you are crazy. However, you can't let this get you down. Whenever you find yourself in a position of being unique, embrace it.

Only you can be you. Your calling is what makes you... you. Be unique! So, today, I challenge you to be different. Be unique. Be you!

**Understand**: In the space provided below, write how different inspires you to climb the ladder to success.

_____

_____

_____

_____

_____

# Day 13
# Seeing Opportunity In Failure

Sometimes, it is hard to admit that we did something wrong, especially when it's even harder to correct it. But that is what we have to do. This is an opportunity to grow and improve and change. Making changes in origami arts is not an easy task to do. It's even harder to create and maintain a business for it. Many people said it was too hard and that I would not be good at it. Even today, I look back at the pictures of my old origami art and am reminded how far I have come. The first origami creation that I can remember making was an origami bird. The first time I made it, it didn't look anything like what was on the computer screen. Yet, that disappointment caused me to keep trying until I got it right.

Let your failures motivate you to succeed. This is a lesson that everyone must learn if they want to be successful. You must not quit if you fail.

So, today, I challenge you to develop undying perseverance. As the old saying goes, "Keep On Keepin' On".

**Understand**: In the space provided below, write how seeing the light in a dark place can help you move higher up the ladder to success

_____

_____

_____

_____

# Day 14
# Don't Write Your Dreams In Pencil

Have you ever written your dreams in pencil? What was it? This question may take some time to answer, so let me break it down. When you write your dreams in pencil, it gives you the chance to erase them. Don't do this! By erasing your dreams, you may be erasing the next big thing from happening.

Write your dreams in pen. When I say "pen", I am not being literal. But when you want to do something in "pencil", it symbolizes that you are only going to do it for a certain season. Pencil symbolizes that the whole idea could be a mistake and tempt you to erase it all way and just rewrite it again in future. However, when you write your dreams in pen, it becomes a permanent thing. It says a lot about your character. It shows that you are a person who knows how to commit to your goals. People that do this succeed because they have determination. Even if they make a mistake, they don't just fall down, they get back up and try again.

So, today, I challenge you to write your dreams in pen. Develop a mindset of perseverance and be committed to your dreams.

**Understand**: In the space provided below, write how completing goals can get you higher up the ladder to success.

_____

_____

# Day 15
# Paying The Bills Of Your Success

You are responsible for paying the bills of your success. This means you must pay the price through your hard work. You must do what it takes to climb the ladder to success. If you look at it in a literal sense, it takes effort to climb a ladder. It's important that we don't confuse "climbing the ladder to success" with the everyday "rat race". Climbing a ladder takes careful movements and patients. People who climb ladders take their time. They are not in a rush and they are not competing with anyone. They never look around. They only look up!

So, today, I challenge you to be ready and willing to pay the bills for your climb. Strive for success, even if you can't see the edge of the ladder or know the outcome.

**Understand**: In the space provided below, write how being responsible for the cost of success is worth the price and how it will help you climb higher up the ladder to success.

_____

_____

_____

_____

_____

_____

# Day 16
# Do What Your Capable Of

Many of us have big dreams, but in order to fulfill those dreams we need to realize what we are capable of doing first. You must figure out what you are interested in doing before anything else. Personally, as an entrepreneur, when I first began there were a large variety of things that I wanted to do. But I first had to look within myself and see what I wanted to pursue the most.

It is good to be passionate about things that we want to pursue, but we have to remember that we can't do everything. If you were to do everything you wanted to do, it would cause you to not put enough effort into those goals. Also, you have to know the difference between a need and a desire. One is always going to be stronger than the other. Balance your needs with your desires. You also need to know your limits as well as limitations. Some you will have to work through. Others you will have to work around. Never let them be your excuse for not succeeding. In any event, your only true limits are only those you place on yourself. If you tell yourself I'm not capable of doing succeeding, you won't succeed.

**Understand**: In the space provided below, write what are some things that you would like to accomplish in life and then explain how knowing what you are capable of can help you get higher up the ladder to success.

_____

_____

_____

_____

# Day 17
# Staying Focused

Staying focused can lead to a lot of positive things. It can cause you to persevere without you even knowing it. Think of it as walking somewhere. As you are walking, you must have a focused mind because if not, you may end up forgetting where you are going.

Some things you can do to stay focused is remembering your destination. For example, studying for a test may be difficult or even boring, but if you want to pass you must study. Setting your mind on a passing grade may help you to study and even motivate you to study harder.

So, today, I challenge you to stay focused. In doing so, you will be motivated to reach your goal.

**Understand**: In the space provided below, write how staying focused help you climb the ladder to success.

_____

_____

_____

_____

_____

_____

_____

# Day 18
# Leading Skills

What is a leader? One simple definition says "a leader is one who leads", but it true leadership is much more than this. One thing that many people don't realize is that in order to be a good leader, you must be influenced by some type of source to lead. In order to lead, especially a group of people, you must always expect the unexpected. This means you must also be a risk taker.

When leading people, you can't be limited to only one plan. A true leader is always prepared for the unexpected. A good leader is also willing to give to his or her followers. Sometimes at their own expense. This isn't an easy task. So when you do lead, keep in mind that, not only is it a difficult job, but also an important one.

So, today, I challenge you to lead and to help others climb to success.

**Understand**: In the space provided below, write what kind of leader you are and how this help will help you climb higher up the ladder to success.

_____

_____

_____

_____

_____

_____

# Day 19
# Seizing Opportunities

Something I like to repeat to myself, time and time again, is "Always take advantage of an opportunity because this opportunity may lead to another better one". The keys to success are temporary but the doors of success are permanent. The keys represent the many ways to become successful. The door represents the success you achieve. Once achieved, no one can take it from you. Think of it like this, if you have a key, you can open a door, but if you don't have a key then it becomes impossible to open the door.

Whenever you find a key to opportunity, be quick to take advantage of it. Use it to open the door of success. Then you can take further steps up the ladder to success,.

So, today, I challenge you to take advantage of any opportunity that may come your way.

**Understand**: In the space provided below, write how taking advantage of opportunities can help you climb up the ladder to success.

_____

_____

_____

_____

_____

# Day 20
## The Power Of Fear

The word fear simply means to be afraid of something or someone. But this is not always the case. This definition stops before a very important part. Being afraid of something or someone can prevent us from pursuing our dreams. Fear is caused by thinking too much. As a result of thinking too much, it causes us to think about our obstacles in trying to do what we want.

Sometimes fear grips us because we are afraid that we are going to fail because of a lack of finances or a lack of skill. This worrying can easily be eliminated by asking for help. Something you must remember is that you can't do everything on your own. Asking for assistance shows that you are humble and not afraid to admit your limitations.

Another thing that causes us to fear is listening to other people's opinion about who we are. If you do feel like your character is being verbally attacked, shut it out of your mind. Don't give in to that energy. I would advise that you reevaluate yourself and remind yourself who you are. It may even take you telling yourself out loud while looking in a mirror saying "I was put on this earth to do great things!".

**Understand**: In the space provided below, write how you can examine yourself so that you can eliminate all fear and how this will help you climb higher up the ladder to success.

_____

_____

_____

# Day 21
# Putting Effort Into Your Dreams

Sometimes in life we are so eager about doing the things we love, that we forget to put time into it. It causes us to rush and try to get everything done all at once. You may know the story of the three little pigs. But if you look a little deeper into this story, you can find a lesson that can affect our lives today. As we all know, two of the three little pigs get their houses blown down and destroyed. Both pigs end up being eaten by the Big Bad Wolf.

In life, we must be sure that we are standing on a sure foundation. If not, when the naysayers come around, we will easily be destroyed. Those two pigs were very eager about building a home that they built it out of weak materials like straw and wood. Sometimes, we tend to build our dreams on weak foundations. Not only does this make people destroy our dreams, but along with the dream, they take away a piece of your heart and soul that can never be restored.

So, today, I not only want to remind you to build your dreams on a strong foundation, but to also to make sure you never give anyone the power to destroy it.

**Understand**: In the space provided below, write how building your dreams will help you climb higher up the ladder to success.

_____

_____

_____

_____

# Day 22
# Feeding Your Dream

I like to think of a dream as a plant. I give it everything it needs to grow and prosper. Many people have very big and positive dreams that could make an impact on this world in unimaginable ways, but the reason why they don't is because they are not feeding their dreams.

In a literal way, the word "feed" means to nourish. As a result of that nourishment, that thing or person will grow. However, the reason why people don't feed their dreams is because they don't know how or what to feed it. In order to feed this dream, they must know when are they are feeding this dream. Having too much of something can be bad for you. So if you feed something too much, you may kill it.

Also, you must know what your are feeding it. If you make it feed off of bad energy, the plant will die. However, if you feed it positive energy, the plant will grow and even multiply. That is why it is crucial to not only have, but to also maintain a positive mindset. As the dream grows, it will become a part of you.

**Understand**: In the space provided below, write how giving your dream proper "nutrients" help you climb the ladder to success.

_____

_____

_____

_____

# Day 23
# Aiming For Perfection

It's not unusual to hear people say, "I'm only human" or "Nobody's perfect". Although they are correct, this is not an excuse to not strive toward that perfection in life.

The truth is when you aim for perfection and shoot your shot at it, you will almost always miss. But with practice you get better and will get ever closer to hitting your target and reaching perfection. Don't give up and never stop aiming. The minute that you do, it you will automatically fail.

Always listen to your conscience and avoid doing wrong. Doing harm to people is not aiming for perfection. Your conscience tells you what is right from wrong. Think and make the right choice. Your ability to improve yourself is what makes you so unique. You have control over your decisions and therefore your success.

No one can climb the ladder to success for you. So, by aiming for perfection, not only are you setting a goal for yourself, but you are making a commitment to climb the ladder to success with skill and perfection.

**Understand**: In the space provided below, write how aiming for perfection can help you climb the ladder to success.

_____

_____

_____

_____

# Day 24
# Making Positive Decisions

You are where you are today because of the decision that you made yesterday. This is why it is important to make good decisions. Every little thing you decide to do now, will affect who you will be tomorrow. If your life is filled with negativity because of the bad decisions of the past, then I have good news for you. It's never too late to change yourself. Positive decisions today result in positive things for the future.

This a problem that many people are facing today. There is a lot of negativity in the world today because of all the bad decisions people made yesterday. Many people don't know that their present condition is a result of negative decisions in the past. And most of these people have no idea that their lives can get better.

When you choose to make right decisions, it helps you to update your life situation. You can go from being a negative person to a positive person. This causes others to look at you differently.

**Understand**: In the space provided below, write how making the right choices helps you climb higher up the ladder to success.

_____

_____

_____

_____

# Day 25
# Perseverance VS. Overdoing

A lot of the time, people say, "Don't give up!" or "Keep trying!" but there is something I want you to realize when listening to this advice. You must remember that you can't do the same thing over and over again and expect a different result. This is the definition of insanity.

Many of us try to build a healthy lifestyle by creating good relationships and eating right. If I eat poorly and surround myself with bad people, I cannot expect a healthy lifestyle. It is impossible to keep doing these things and expect a different result. However, you can cross over to a better life through perseverance.

Perseverance is sticking with a task until you achieve your goal. Never confuse this with what I call overdoing. Overdoing is doing the same thing and expecting a different result. Overdoing is insanity.

If you want a different result, you need to make a different strategy. This is why I encourage people to do new things and get out of their comfort zones. When people do this, it gives them the opportunity to discover something new.

**Understand**: In the space provided below, write how perseverance can help you climb higher up the ladder to success.

_____

_____

_____

_____

# Day 26
# Avoid A Climbing Competition

Each and every one of us has a gift, a talent, and a skill. No gift is greater or smaller than any other. The use of the gift determines the greatness of it. That being said, climbing up your ladder to success is not a competition. How fast or slow you get there doesn't matter. Climbing up the ladder to success isn't a competition. It's a journey.

We must not pit our gifts and talents against someone else's gifts and talents. Otherwise, we all lose. We lose ourselves and remembering why we started this climb in the first place.

I would encourage you to climb united. This journey won't be easy, so find a group of people are willing to climb with you. People who can motivate you when your strength is failing. So, today, I challenge you to quit the competition and look for companions. Together you can both climb even higher up the ladder to success.

**Understand**: In the space provided below, write how you can apply this to your life and climb higher up the ladder to success.

_____

_____

_____

_____

_____

# Day 27
# Your Steps On The Ladder

If you didn't know, consider this... There is no end to the ladder to success. No matter what you do or how you do it, there will always be room for improvement. No matter how hard we try, there is always something we can do better.

For this reason, today, I want you to plan your success. Remember that organization is worthless if it is connected to procrastination. Hold yourself accountable to how serious you are when it comes to climbing. Keeping a written record will make your life better and help you to become more successful.

Start by writing out the following:

1. My success or goal is..

2. How and When will I accomplish it

3. The steps I need to take every day to reach this goal

    is...


**Understand**: In the space provided below, write how can being organized help me get higher up the ladder to success.

_____

_____

# Day 28
# The Importance Of Looking Down

Most motivational speakers tell people to "Keep your head up!" While that is good advice, it is also important to look down at times. Looking up at where your dream is and where your success is taking you can sometimes blind you to important things like being grateful and appreciating family. Look down every now and then. Make sure your feet are not wavering off the path to your success. Realign your feet with your purpose.

Sometimes, in life, we need to acquaint ourselves with people that will remind us to realign our feet when we really need it. In today's society, most success people have a tendency to keep their head up in the clouds. They don't realize it, but staring at the "sun" of their success, money, and fame is blinding them from their true purpose.

So, today, I challenge you to take a glimpse down for a second. Evaluate your character. If it doesn't align with your purpose, then I encourage you to realign your footsteps with your purpose.

**Understand**: In the space provided below, write how looking down helps you climb higher up the ladder to success.

_____

_____

_____

_____

_____

# Day 29
# The Shield Of Positivity

People who fight fire with fire end up getting burned. You can't fight wrong with wrong or bad with bad. Let's look at paint as an illustration. When you mix yellow paint with yellow paint, all you get is a bigger blob of yellow paint. However, when you mix red paint and yellow paint, you get a whole different color. You get a beautiful color called orange.

One of the many, many problems in today's world is that people don't understand the power of positivity. Since we see negativity all around us on TV and on our tablets it creates more of an impact than positivity. To make it worse when people say something bad to us, we have an urge to say something negative back to them.

Here's an equation I use to explain this:

**Positivity > Negativity**
**Negativity < Positivity**

Some people fail to realize that even though positivity is greater, negativity still has power which causes them to not work to the best of their ability. While climbing higher up your ladder to success, there will be people throwing stones at you. So, today, I challenge you to not throw them back. Instead throw them something positivity for a change.

**Understand**: In the space provided below, write how knowing the value of positivity can help you climb higher up the ladder to success.

_____

_____

_____

_____

_____

_____

_____

_____

_____

_____

_____

_____

_____

_____

_____

_____

_____

# Day 30
# You Need Turbulence and Delays

Just like on an airplane, our lives can experience some turbulence and delays. If you have ever experienced really bad turbulence on an airplane, then you were probably terrified. You may have even been awakened from your sleep. However, despite how it looks, we need turbulence and delays to reach success. These troubles in life help us stay alert and vigilant. It also helps use develop a proper appreciation when our success arrives.

Think of it as a hot air balloon. This balloon requires helium and heat to lift off the ground. Sometimes our lives seems stuck between a rock in a hard place. Instead of sitting in despair, we need to turn up the heat so we can rise above our troubles and get elevated to the next level.

Success is not a gift. It has to be fought for and doesn't come easy. Opportunities may be handed to you but you have to work hard to make them successful. So, when turbulence and delays come your way, don't be discouraged. Just keep in mind that these troubles are tools that can be used to elevate you to the next level of success.

**Understand**: In the space provided below, write how understanding turbulence and delays are necessary to help you climb higher up the ladder to success.

_____

_____

_____

_____

# Day 31
# True Success

A lot of people ask me, how did I achieve so much success in such a short period of time? The answer to that comes from knowing what success truly is. Contrary to popular belief, success isn't being famous or having wealth. True success is a feeling of satisfaction within yourself. The only way to feel that satisfaction within yourself is by accomplishing what you want to accomplish in life. However, your accomplishments should not define your character. Your accomplishments are only a small part of your success.

The second you become a true winner, you can automatically achieve success. As I mentioned on the very first day of this daily climb, you can become a true winner by reaching your goal. The only way to feel satisfied in this life is if you find fulfillment in yourself. You can consider yourself successful if you make a million dollars, but true success isn't about being rich and famous. True success comes from doing what you love doing and doing it well.

So, today, as you complete this final day of your daily climb, I encourage you to keep on climbing the ladder to success. I challenge you to examine yourself. Put yourself on a "detox" cleanse. Clean out all the things that make you miserable in life. Now go out there and make your dream come true.

**Understand**: In the space provided below, write out what you can do every day to climb higher up the ladder to success.

_____

_____

# *"Believe in yourself"*

If you liked this book by Denar Ralph

then check out his first book

Climbing The Ladder To Success: Just A Little Inspiration
ISBN 978-1-387-40476-6

# ABOUT THE AUTHOR

Denar was born on January 7, 2005 to Denroy and Patricia Ralph. Approximately eleven months before his birth, both of his parents were told by the doctor that they would not have any more children due to a battle with prostate cancer. As you can see, the doctors were very wrong. What the devil meant for bad, God turned it around for His good. He is here today with a message to encourage and inspire others. He draws strength and courage from the writings of the ancients. His favorite comes from a Roman prisoner called Paul of Tarsus who wrote, "I can do all things through Christ who strengthens me." His mission in life is to "change lives and help realize that they too can do anything that they put their minds to.

# MISSION
## Three-Six-Teens
# 3:16

### Youth Ministry